# Sharks

## Jeffrey C. Carrier

Voyageur Press

# Contents

Introducing the Shark — 5

What Makes a Shark 'a Shark'? — 9
Shark Skin — 11
Shark Teeth — 12
Where did the Earliest Sharks Come From? — 12
How many Different Kinds of Sharks Are There? — 13
Shark Oddities — 14
Where are Sharks Found? — 17
Is there a Standard Shark Shape? — 17

Shark Survival — 21
What do Sharks Eat and How do they Feed? — 21
Why are Sharks such Effective Predators? — 22
Do Sharks See, Smell or Hear their Prey? — 23
How Fast do Sharks Grow? — 26
How Long do Sharks Live? — 28
How Far do Sharks Move during their Lives? — 28

Shark Behavior — 31
What do we Know about Shark Behavior? — 31
Shark Attacks — 32
How do Sharks Reproduce? — 34
How Long are Sharks Pregnant? — 38

Sharks & the Environment — 41
Are Sharks Valuable? — 41

Index — 48

# Introducing the Shark

The beginning of April in the shallow, crystal-clear waters of the Florida Keys is always a wondrous time. The subtle drop in water temperature that accompanies what passes for winter in this sub-tropical region gives way to the rising temperatures of spring. Even aquatic life seems to bloom to welcome the new season. For sportfishers the warming waters bring forth the game fish that use the inshore shallows as nursery grounds.

Fish such as tarpon, bonefish, and permit, much sought-after prizes in the world of saltwater trophy fishing, make their first appearances of the new year. The inshore seagrass beds teem with life and support one of the richest aquatic nursery grounds known.

These nearshore habitats and the adjacent offshore coral reefs attract a diverse assemblage of marine animals in numbers that are astounding, even to marine biologists. Such underwater realms rival terrestrial ecosystems such as tropical rain forests in their biodiversity and species density. And where there are large numbers of fish and crustaceans and

*BLACKTIP REEF SHARKS*
*Sharks are found in abundance in tropical seas and are frequently encountered on coral reefs around the world. The large diversity of animal species and the dense populations of reef fish provide ample food supplies for cruising sharks.*

*SANDBAR SHARK (left)*

**NURSE SHARK**

*The placement of the paired pectoral and pelvic fins along the underside of sharks provides lift – much like the wings of airplanes – to these animals that have no mechanism to control their buoyancy. Since they have no swim bladder like most other fish, they must swim to change their depth in the water and their fins help to accomplish this movement.*

mollusks that one associates with the richest marine habitats, there will most certainly be large numbers of predatory fish and, of course, the foremost predator among them – the shark.

It is this dizzying array of animals and the sharks that prey upon them that brings me to the Florida Keys every year. For nearly 40 years I have studied sharks in these pristine waters, concentrating on what is perhaps the most often encountered species in these tropical shallows, the nurse shark. Even as a youngster growing up along the northeastern coast of Florida, the lure of these mysterious and misunderstood sea serpents was enough to coax me away from classes, much to the dismay of my teachers, who despaired of my apparent disregard of more traditional studies. Try as they might, they never quite understood my preference for all things aquatic, especially those creatures with large fins and toothy grins.

The onset of spring signals the reappearance of sharks in these shallow waters as they follow the lead of other species seeking the refuge of the more protected inshore waters. They follow these other species in part to dine, in part to mate, as thoughts of spring tantalize even sharks. Biologists are able to take advantage of sharks that use nearshore shallow waters, for they are easier to observe, easier to track, and easier to capture for studies of growth, aging, and reproduction.

Though our preferred research species is the nurse shark, the tropics are home to many other species that also frequent the shallow waters. Hammerhead sharks with their bizarre, flattened heads, tiger sharks, with artistic color patterns that rival airbrush artists in their detail and flow of color, and countless other species also appear more frequently in the early spring. It is the stunning diversity of these immensely successful fish that we welcome back every year. Their reappearance causes us to continually marvel at their success and to wonder just how these animals have survived for nearly 400 million years. What features confer such a survival advantage over other aquatic animals? How are the nearly 400 species different from each

other? What makes them so ideally suited for their ecosystematic role as apex predators? Will they persist through time as the most feared 'denizen of the deep?' Or do they have their own enemies that threaten their very existence in ways that nature has been unsuccessful for millennia? How do humans relate and interact with sharks? What are scientists discovering about sharks and their value to the ecosystem and to humankind?

To understand sharks means that we must first understand something of their diversity and evolution, and those special attributes that make a shark 'a shark.' We begin the process of discovering sharks.

*TIGER SHARK*

*Even sharks have their 'enemies'. Many different parasites are found associated with sharks. Some strange crustaceans are found on shark eyes, giving them the appearance of very strange eyelashes. Others are found in their gill cavities or in their mouths. None of these are fatal to sharks.*

# What Makes a Shark 'a Shark'?

Biologists are forever devising schemes to classify plants and animals and to tell the difference between species. What have they discovered about sharks that makes them different from other fishes?

Most fishes that people encounter belong to the very large group that are called 'bony' fishes because their skeleton is made of true bone, a very complex mixture of calcium and other elements, which is also very rigid. Sharks lack true bone. Instead their skeleton is made of cartilage, a very flexible substance that is also the substance of human ears and noses. This flexibility may even aid the shark in swimming: as the shark moves its tail from side to side, the flexibility of cartilage may help to 'snap' the tail back at the end of each swimming stroke, thus requiring less energy from skeletal muscles.

Most aquatic animals use gills to obtain oxygen from the water in the process of respiration. Marine mammals such as dolphins and whales are the exceptions. Instead of gills, they use lungs similar to those of land animals. Gills perform the same role as lungs. Oxygen moves from the water into the fish and waste products such as carbon dioxide leave the fish across the gills. This aquatic respiration requires that the water around the gills be constantly moved, either by using muscles around the gills to move water through the fish's mouth and across the gills,

**SEVEN-GILL SHARK**

*The teeth of sharks are often lost in the violence of feeding. Studies have shown that teeth are produced as long as the shark lives and new teeth can quickly replace ones that are lost. But the teeth are not the only problem that may result from a shark encounter. Shark skin is covered with microscopic scales that resemble teeth. A brush with a swimming shark can leave some severe scrapes.*

**GREAT WHITE SHARK (left)**

**SILVERTIP SHARK**

*Shark reproductive strategies do not prepare them well to survive modern-day fishing pressures and technologies. They generally grow very slowly and mature late in their lives. They do not produce the large number of offspring that bony fish produce. These shortcomings doom heavily fished populations and only prudent management strategies can protect populations at risk.*

or by constantly swimming with the mouth slightly open. Fish have a thin bony plate called an 'operculum' that covers the gills. Muscles attach the operculum to the mouth and the jaw muscles so that fish can draw water in through the mouth and across the gills, constantly moving the water to aid in respiration. Sharks lack an operculum. Their gills are open to the outside through gill 'slits,' five in almost all species (except for six-gilled and seven-gilled sharks).

Because sharks lack this special structure, most species cannot create currents that bring water across the gills. Instead they must constantly swim with their mouths open – for their entire lives – in order to allow the water to cross the gills so they can effectively 'breathe.' Some species, mostly bottom-dwelling sharks such as the nurse shark, do have the capability to create these water currents on their own and can therefore remain motionless on the sea floor. But most species have to swim in order to breathe, mouths slightly open with teeth exposed, giving them an ominous appearance as though they are always ready to strike.

Bony fishes possess a gas-filled bag – often thought to resemble a lung

– that is used by the fish to control its vertical position in the water. This structure is called a swim bladder. If it is filled with air by the fish, the fish can rise in the water. If it is emptied of air, the fish will sink. Sharks lack a swim bladder. The only way they can control their position in the water – the depth where they are found – is to swim there; they cannot come to the surface unless they swim to it. Most sharks also weigh more than the water that surrounds them. They are said to be 'negatively buoyant.' Oils in the liver may provide a little buoyancy and some sharks actually gulp air at the surface to provide buoyancy. But, in general, if sharks stop swimming, they will sink. They will also suffocate, since they require the constant movement of water across their gills in order to breathe. It should come as no surprise, then, that sharks are well equipped with features that make them effective swimmers.

Fins in fish are useful for controlling swimming movements. The tail fin (caudal fin) is the main structure and it provides the thrust to move the fish. The fins atop the fish, the 'dorsal fins,' help to keep the fish upright in the water, much like the keel of a boat. The paired fins found on the sides of fishes have other roles. The pair on the front of the fish near the gill area is called the 'pectoral' fins and the pair of fins toward the back of the fish is called the 'pelvic' fins. In bony fish, the pectoral fins may be used to propel the fish and allow them to move backwards or forward. In sharks, both of these pairs of fins are located near the bottom of the body and not on the sides of the animals, as occur in bony fish. They are also much more rigid. Their role in sharks is to serve as 'diving' planes and control lift. By using these fins, a swimming shark controls whether it rises in the water or sinks to deeper water, much in the same way that airplanes and submarines control whether they climb or dive.

## Shark Skin

Even the skin of a shark is different from that of other fishes. The skin's surface is covered with what appear to be millions of tiny teeth when viewed under a microscope. They are actually more like teeth than the thin, circular scales seen on most other types of fish. They are thought to reduce friction and drag as the shark swims, though they can inflict a serious wound on an unsuspecting swimmer who brushes against a fast-moving shark. These 'skin teeth' or 'dermal denticles' seem to be different for different shark species. The thickened, flat denticles shown above are from nurse sharks, which favor living on the bottom, often under sharp coral formations.

## Shark Teeth

The teeth of sharks show as much variability as the sharks themselves. They are generally suited for the particular prey that sharks seek. Some are straight, some are very crooked, and some are flattened. Bottom-dwelling sharks, which feed on crustaceans like shrimp and lobsters or mollusks with their hard shells, have teeth that are well suited for crushing prey. Sharks that feed on fish generally have more pointed teeth to hold onto fish that have been captured. The cookie-cutter shark is among the most unusual sharks. Its mouth and jaw are structured so that when it bites a chunk of flesh from its prey, it leaves an almost perfectly round hole.

Finally, the one characteristic that most people first associate with sharks is their teeth. Teeth are one of the few structures in sharks that are well-hardened and last for long periods of time after leaving the animal. A shark at any time will have many teeth that are present in rows under their 'gums.' When a tooth is lost in feeding, or for any other reason, a replacement will roll forward in the jaw in a matter of days to replace the lost tooth. There is always a newly formed tooth to roll forward and fill the gap from a missing or lost tooth and this process will continue for the entire life of the animal.

## Where did the Earliest Sharks Come From?

The very characteristics that make a shark a shark also make understanding their early origins and ancestors very complicated. Cartilage, their main skeletal component, does not preserve well in fossils. This means that the earliest forms of sharks have been reconstructed using the only body parts that do fossilize well, the teeth or hard spines.

Though there are some exceptional fossil remains of wholly intact ancient sharks, most remains that have been discovered are teeth or tooth fragments. From these remains, very bizarre ancestral sharks have been reconstructed. While they may seem strange in appearance and not at all like modern sharks, they shared the same biological characteristics that are seen in today's living sharks. Sophisticated laboratory analyses have revealed that these earliest sharks were probably present in a time known as the Devonian, nearly 400 million years ago. Some sharks, now long extinct, may have resembled the modern-day great white shark and may have reached lengths of more than 52 ft (16 m), more than twice the length of what are thought to be the largest great whites of today. If a 52 ft (16 m) long shark with an attitude of a modern-day great white is not enough to make even an experienced shark-chaser take note, imagine triangular, razor-sharp teeth that are larger than a large man's hand. Such mammoth fossils have been discovered from many fossil sites.

## How many Different Kinds of Sharks Are There?

The best estimates of the total number of sharks suggest that between 375 and 400 different species exist today. The total number is always changing because of two important advances in technology: deep-sea exploration and modern techniques in cell and molecular biology. The newest types of deep-sea submersibles and remote video cameras have made the ocean depths more accessible. Using these tools, species of sharks never seen before have been discovered in recent years.

Additionally, new laboratory procedures have allowed scientists to compare DNA taken from sharks in various parts of the world to determine how closely related different species may be to each other. Many species of sharks closely resemble other sharks in appearance. Often even experts may be incorrect in their identification unless an animal has been captured and can be examined closely. Comparisons

*ANCESTRAL SHARKS*

*Ancestral sharks are probably best known for their bizarre body shapes and strange jaws. With teeth on wheels and strange projections from their heads, it's difficult to believe these were living fish and not the result of some artistic paleontologist's imagination.*

## Shark Oddities

Some species seem oddly deformed when compared to the typical shark. Foremost among these would be the hammerhead sharks with their strangely flattened head. Scientists are not certain whether there is a specific function of such a flattened head. Many agree that the larger spacing of the shark's eyes and nostrils (called 'nares' in sharks), as well as other finely developed sensory systems, may assist the hammerhead in locating prey more effectively. Hammerhead sharks may also be able to more rapidly adjust their swimming movements by using the head as a hydrofoil, a device that allows them to dive or ascend more quickly through the water. To encounter one underwater is exhilarating as well as somewhat startling. They seem to be able to turn in a space of mere inches and can change direction in the blink of an eye, challenging the diver to be constantly alert.

of DNA between closely related species may help scientists determine whether two similar animals are the same species, because their DNA is nearly identical, or if they are different species.

Another problem that complicates identification is that sharks may have different common names in different parts of the world. For example, a bull shark may be called a 'cub' shark, a 'ground' shark, a 'Zambezi River' shark, or a 'Lake Nicaragua' shark, depending on where one might be encountered. To a biologist, these are probably the same species, *Carcharhinus leucas*. The bull shark may be a good example to illustrate why the use of Latin species names is so valuable. A single species has one and only one Latin name instead of many common names. In this way, scientists can communicate without the risk of discussing what may be very different species. There must be at least 25 different species of sharks that are all referred to by beach-goers and fishers as 'sand' sharks, making communication very difficult!

Sharks are closely related to two other commonly encountered groups of animals: the skates and rays. These groups also include the strange and increasingly rare sawfish and the more common stingrays. Sharks are also relatives of the rare and mostly extinct chimaeras, though

*ANGEL SHARK (top)*
*LEOPARD SHARK (bottom)*

*SAW SHARK (top)*
*ZEBRA (LEOPARD) SHARK (bottom)*

**SILKY SHARK**

*A skeleton made of cartilage instead of bone provides enhanced flexibility as sharks seem to move through the water with little effort.*

the focus here will be on the more recognizable group that are commonly known as the sharks.

## Where are Sharks Found?

Sharks are found worldwide. They range from tropical waters to Arctic seas, from the ocean depths to waters barely knee deep, from near-shore habitats to the open ocean. They are mostly marine (saltwater), but some have been found in freshwater lakes and rivers. They range in size from animals that are fully mature and fully grown at 10 in (25 cm) (the pygmy shark) to those that may reach lengths in excess of 40 to 50 ft (12 to 15 m). At this length, the whale shark is the largest 'fish' in the sea. Most species, however, seldom grow to 7 ft (2 m) in total length. In fact, nearly 50 per cent of all shark species never reach more than 3 ft 6 in (1 m) in length and 82 per cent never reach 7 ft (2 m) in length.

## Is there a Standard Shark Shape?

The typical shark has a torpedo-shaped body that is ideally suited for swimming at the higher speeds necessary to chase down fast-swimming prey items like fish. Most people who have some familiarity with sharks

*WHALE SHARK*

*Seen from the head, some of the larger sharks, like whale sharks, appear more whale-like than shark-like, though the dorsal fins and tail soon reveal their true identities. Other sharks, such as the hammerheads, just seem to defy any design criteria!*

**WOBBEGONG SHARK**

*Most sharks, especially those that inhabit the open ocean, are easily recognized by their streamlined, torpedo shapes. But not all species follow the same design template. Bottom-dwelling sharks such as the angel shark and Australia's wobbegong shark are flattened and even covered with flaps and folds of skin that provide some camouflage, hiding them from unsuspecting prey.*

**BASKING SHARK (right)**

*The massive basking shark actually dines on the ocean's smallest organisms, the plankton, needing to filter tons of water through their gaping mouths to extract a single meal.*

from television think first of the great white shark as the 'typical' shark. Many spectators who visit the world's aquaria and see captive shark displays have seen brown sharks, also called sandbar sharks, or the sand tiger shark, also called the ragged tooth shark, and they have formed their image of sharks from these species.

But many sharks have bodies that are oddly bizarre and appear very unlike a typical shark. The Australian wobbegong shark and some carpet sharks have flaps of skin that offer them some camouflage and prevent them from being spotted by unsuspecting prey. Often these species are better suited to living on the sea floor and feed on shrimps, lobsters, or mollusks rather than fish. The huge basking sharks with their giant mouths, often wide open to strain microscopic planktonic prey from the water, might easily be confused with whales by those unfamiliar with the differences between sharks and whales. These very largest of the sea creatures feed on the very same food sources, plankton, the smallest of the sea's plants and animals.

Other sharks, such as the diminutive epaulette shark and the leopard shark, appear to have been painted by a master airbrush artist. Their colorful patterns offer a disruptive coloration that may also provide some camouflage by masking their shark-like forms.

No discussion of shark oddities would be complete without mention of the thresher shark, whose tail may actually exceed the length of its body. Thresher sharks feed by slashing through schools of food fish, disabling them with their powerful tails, and then returning to feed on fish that have been stunned by this bizarre behavior.

# Shark Survival

## What do Sharks Eat and How do they Feed?

Someone unfamiliar with the large variety of sharks might expect that all sharks are flesh eaters, silently stalking anything in the sea. Many species are considered to be opportunistic feeders, eating whatever they might encounter. Some species prefer fish. Others might prefer large marine mammals like seals and sea lions.

Many sharks are not as dramatic in their feeding. Some have strong jaws for crushing prey with very small teeth and will feed on crustaceans like lobster, shrimp, and crabs, and can even crush the shells of mollusks like clams and snails. Others can actually remove the snail from the shell by suction feeding! Still others feed on plankton, straining massive amounts of these smallest marine plants and animals from the water. Many species, regardless of their particular preference, may still scavenge weakened, injured, or dead fish and their feeding is hardly spectacular. However in recent years, stunning video taken by researchers and professional film makers has shown that even huge sharks, like adult great white sharks, often come completely out of the water when feeding on prey items on the surface.

Examining the stomach contents of dead sharks can often be surprising. The remains of sea birds, marine turtles, and almost every other type of marine animal have been discovered. There are even reports of stomachs containing dogs, cats, and cattle! If that's not bizarre enough, there are

*GREAT WHITE SHARK*

*The great white shark epitomizes the fearsome shark. The late Peter Benchley's novel* Jaws, *about a vengeful white shark, changed the attitudes of millions of people, who could not walk along the shore without thinking of large fish stalking them from the ocean's depths. Fortunately the great white's value to the ecosystem has now been realized and worldwide efforts to protect this vulnerable species have been enacted.*

*BRONZE WHALERS, OR COPPER SHARKS, FEEDING ON SARDINES (left)*

**GRAY REEF SHARK**

*Just behind the eyes are the gill slits, normally five in number. Water enters a shark's mouth as it swims and leaves through the gill slits after oxygen is absorbed into the body and carbon dioxide and other wastes are lost from the body across the gills. Most sharks must swim continuously to breathe using this method of breathing, which is called ram ventilation. Since they have no swim bladder they must either swim, or sink to the bottom. Some species, however, have developed the ability to rest on the bottom and pull water in and across the gills without the need to swim.*

also reports – maybe some more myth than truth – of finding automobile license plates, aluminum beverage cans, and even a suit of armor!

## Why are Sharks such Effective Predators?

Sharks are among the world's most effective predators. What makes them so successful in discovering food is a very well-developed sensory system that gives them advantages over their intended prey. While they have many of the same sensory systems that are present in most animals, these systems are highly suited to serve them well in an underwater world. They even possess a sensory system that is not seen in terrestrial animals, which helps them to detect animals by sensing the weak electrical currents that are produced by nerves and muscles in living organisms.

Sharks have often been called 'swimming noses' because of their keen sense of smell ('olfaction'). Some estimates suggest that 20 to 30 per cent of the shark's brain may be devoted to its sense of smell. Though there is some disagreement of just how sensitive their sense of smell may be (1 part per million, 1 part per billion, etc.), most are agreed that they can detect minute traces of attractive chemicals in the water. Some of these chemicals may indicate food items and may lead to a searching behavior. Some substances, such as blood, may signal a wounded animal and an easy target. Other substances ('pheromones') may signal that a mate is nearby and bring about an entirely different response. The fact that sharks can detect such small quantities of chemicals may explain why they can be attracted from very long distances as they follow an

# Do Sharks See, Smell or Hear their Prey?

A logical question to ask is, 'What sensory system is the most important as the shark tracks its prey?' Any good biologist would try to avoid giving a direct answer by saying that it depends on the intensity of the stimulus, that is, how much sound is being generated, or how much blood is in the water or how clear is the water? It should be clear that every situation is likely to be slightly different. A thrashing swimmer or fish that is bleeding from a wound in very clear water may be at risk since all of the shark's sensory systems could work well.

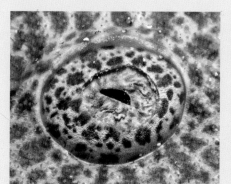
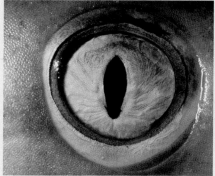

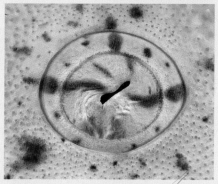

Other circumstances could be more confusing for the shark, but easier for a human to understand. For example, most reported shark attacks occur in the surf very near beaches. In these situations, a shark could not see well because the water is generally very turbid. The senses of smell and hearing would not work well either, since the odors would be disturbed from the crashing waves and the sounds would be equally confusing. In fact, most scientists agree that encounters with sharks near the seashore are probably results of mistakes by the shark. They may encounter a swimmer and simply respond by biting without really being certain of the identity of the target, and then they rapidly swim away. Though likely a case of mistaken identity, the shark is rarely forgiven for its accidental encounters.

The shark's sensory systems are well suited to its role as a top predator. It is able to detect sounds in the low-frequency range, the same sounds that are produced by wounded fish or struggling swimmers. Sharks are also able to see well in dim light because of reflective layers in the back of the eyes, adaptations that are similar to those of cats, an advantage over prey that might not see so well. The keen sense of smell combined with these other sensory systems makes the shark ideally suited to detect and stalk its prey.

**BLACKTIP SHARK**

*Sharks are characterized by marine ecologists as apex predators, those animals that live at the top the marine food chain. Their keen sensory systems equip them well for that role and, with the exception of other sharks and some of the large, toothed whales, they have few natural predators.*

odor corridor. Fishers take advantage of this sensory ability of sharks by placing large quantities of fish meal or blood in the water (called 'chum') to attract sharks. Even though greatly diluted by ocean currents, the shark can detect small quantities of these substances and follow the odor trail to its source.

The sense of hearing in sharks is remarkably well adapted for aiding in the detection and location of food. Most scientific studies in the laboratory and in the field conclude that sharks hear well in the very low-frequency ranges, much the same type of sound that would be associated with a struggling fish or some other wounded animal. This would be useful for any predator and might help to locate food that requires less energy to capture because of its injuries. It is worth noting that the sounds made by wounded fish are similar to the sounds thought to be made by a struggling swimmer – one of the reasons why a quiet retreat is recommended for those who are in the water with sharks and who are attempting to get out of the water!

The shark's visual system also seems to be well suited for that of a predator. The eyes of most species of shark seem to be capable of color vision and their vision is thought to be fairly sharp ('visual acuity'), though only about one-tenth of that in humans. In addition, sharks may be able to tell the difference between object shapes. Their eyes are also equipped with a reflective layer called a *tapetum lucidum*, which may amplify light under dim conditions, much like that of nocturnal predators like cats. This feature enables sharks to see in low light conditions, such as dawn and dusk, when their targets may not see as clearly. How far away sharks can see may be more of a function of the clarity of the water than the effectiveness of their eyes. Some species actually possess a protective eyelid called a nictitating membrane which may close down over the eye to protect it when the shark is feeding.

Perhaps the least well-known shark sensory system is their ability to detect weak electrical voltages. Every animal produces small electrical voltages when nerves fire or when muscles contract. Though these voltages are very small, perhaps only 0.1 volts, they can be detected by an unusual electroreceptor system in sharks. In saltwater, small voltages like these would not travel very far. The ability to detect them at close range might be useful for a shark swimming over a food item that is buried under the sand. This sense might also be useful for closing in on live food items in the final stages of an attack, when the jaw is wide open and the eyes might be closed.

Some unusual, but very well-designed and novel laboratory experiments showed that sharks whose eyes had been covered with patches and whose nostrils had been plugged with cotton soaked in an anesthetic – so the animals were temporarily unable to see and could not smell their prey – could still locate living animals hiding under the sand. If a dead animal was substituted in place of the live animal (one that could no longer produce the electrical voltages that a live animal would produce), the shark was not able to find it. If the 'dead' animal was replaced with electrodes that produced voltages that were the same

*GRAY REEF SHARKS*

*Gray reef sharks feeding off the Marshall Islands, Micronesia, Pacific Ocean. Social organization in shark populations is not well studied. Schools of sharks are often encountered; perhaps they have gathered to hunt, perhaps to mate, perhaps to migrate. What controls how the schools assemble and move is still a mystery.*

25

*SAND TIGER SHARK*

*The sand tiger or 'ragged tooth' shark presents a menacing appearance but is considered by divers and fishermen to be docile and non-threatening. Despite being harmless, they have suffered such severe human persecution, they are now a protected species. In Australia, they are also known as gray nurse sharks even though they are not related to the true nurse sharks.*

as those produced by a living animal, the shark would eat the electrodes!

More recent studies of this electroreception sense are revealing that the long distance that some species of sharks are known to migrate may be in response to the weak electric fields associated with the earth ('geomagnetic navigation'). Their ability to detect these magnetic fields and interpret them in some unknown fashion may assist them in long-distance movement. It is also possible that electric fields generated by other sharks may be detected in low light conditions and help other sharks to identify a mate, particularly in deeper, dark waters where it may be harder to recognize other animals.

## How Fast do Sharks Grow?

Though sharks have been kept in captivity since very early times, little was known of their day-to-day activities and behaviors until the last 20 to 30 years. Studies conducted by scientists and shark fishers worldwide began to show movement patterns and growth rates that were previously unknown. These pieces of information became known because scientists and fishers began to tag sharks with external tags that were easily spotted by other fishers or scientists. Pioneered by the United States National Marine Fisheries Service, sharks were tagged and their length, weight, sex, and location of capture were noted at the time of tagging.

When a tagged shark was later captured by a fisher or scientist, a note and address on the tag requested that the same information – length, weight, sex, and location of capture – be sent to laboratories in Rhode Island where the data were recorded for future analysis.

What emerged from analyses of these early studies, and many more recent studies, surprised scientists by showing that shark growth was very slow. Sharks, like any other animal, must reach certain sizes before they are mature and can reproduce.

For example, the nurse sharks that I study in the Florida Keys with my research colleague, Wes Pratt, grow only 4 to 6 in (10 to 15 cm) per year. They are only 12 in (30 cm) when they are born. The females must reach about 8 ft (230 cm) before they are mature and the males must reach about 7 ft (210 cm). Some simple math shows that these animals are probably nearly 20 years old before they can produce more sharks. Some species grow faster than nurse sharks and some grow more slowly, but this generally slow rate of growth and late maturity may not be characteristics that will serve sharks well in the future if fishing pressures for sharks continue to increase.

*NURSE SHARKS*

*The skin of some shark species is highly valued for its leather-like properties. Once the tooth-like scales are removed from a shark, the remaining skin can be processed and made into a fine grade of leather. Belts, shoes, and other items command a high price for a beautiful grade of leather that lasts for years.*

## How Long do Sharks Live?

No one is quite certain how long sharks live. The evidence suggests that sandbar sharks may live longer than 25 years. Other species may outlive the biologists who study them! If our nurse sharks' growth rates are believed (and we have captured some tagged animals more than five times, so we are pretty confident that our growth and aging estimates are accurate) the males would be nearly 20 when they finally are old enough to mate. In our studies of nurse-shark mating, we tag and photograph every animal that we can. One large and important male ('Notch') has been present and involved in mating activities for 15 years. If he was really 20 years old when we first saw him, he would now be at least 35 years old. Larger species of sharks such as whale sharks, basking sharks, and Greenland sharks, may live considerably longer. They are very difficult to catch and tag, so studies of their growth and aging have not been completed.

## How Far do Sharks Move during their Lives?

Tagging and recapture studies also began to reveal that some species of sharks were very nomadic, some even crossing entire oceans. Blue sharks tagged off the eastern coast of North America were often recaptured off the southern coasts of Europe. Others were captured off South America, showing movements between hemispheres.

Some tagged sharks were recaptured after incredibly long periods between tagging and recapture. One sandbar shark was recaptured nearly 26 years after it was originally tagged, showing not only a long life span for the shark, but a long life span for the tag! The factors that trigger or influence migration in sharks may be the same factors that influence migration in other animals: changing climates, changing or moving food sources, movements to or from mating or nursery grounds, or some combination of all these factors. Seasonal migrations of sharks are well known and often reported by the media in almost hysterical terms: 'Sharks massing off the Florida coast' or 'Increasing populations of sharks menace swimmers.' In fact, these seasonal movements are normal occurrences and are no more threatening than the increases in anchovy or herring or bluefish schools that often precede the sharks.

Recent studies have used tags of a different sort to track shark movements in a less random fashion than relying on recapturing a tagged shark from a huge ocean. Some modern electronic tags can be attached to sharks and can communicate with satellites. In this way, the tags can send information directly to the scientists at their desks, revealing movements of sharks almost instantaneously.

Other types of electronic tags are attached to sharks that move very little – miles instead of hundreds of miles. They can be tracked for short durations by scientists in small boats or can be detected by special receivers anchored to the sea floor in areas where sharks are known to reside for longer periods of time.

These special receivers can simultaneously store information for many different sharks and may be able to receive data for as long as one year without changing batteries. The transmitters that are attached to sharks may also last for a long time. These newer types of technology promise to reveal much more about short-term and local shark movements than has ever been seen before.

**BLUE SHARKS**

*Blue sharks with their vibrant blue color and long pectoral fins are also long-distance swimmers. Tagging studies have shown that they are capable of crossing entire oceans and have even been shown to move from northern to southern hemispheres. Their color allows them to blend in well in the open ocean, and they often emerge like some aquatic ghost.*

# Shark Behavior

## What do we Know about Shark Behavior?

Though many aspects of shark behavior have been studied for the last 60 years, it is still amazing how little we actually know about these long-lived, reclusive animals. Among the first studies were examinations of shark behavior in the presence of substances thought to repel sharks. In the early 1940s, during World War II, scientists under the leadership of Dr. Perry Gilbert, one of the field's most respected investigators, attempted to find substances that would repel sharks and keep them from attacking downed pilots or victims of shipboard disasters. These first studies actually discovered that rotting shark flesh had some repellant powers. The first repellants incorporated some of these compounds into bars that were dissolved in water to create a cloud that supposedly repelled sharks. Later studies showed these first attempts to be largely ineffective.

Dr. Eugenie Clark, a scientist at Cape Haze Marine Laboratory, which later became the Mote Marine Laboratory in Sarasota, Florida, was able to condition lemon and nurse sharks to ring a bell for food. Even more remarkable than the training, the sharks were able to remember this task after intervals of several months when they weren't 'tested.' Dr. Clark also evaluated the ability of sharks to detect different shapes and patterns and was able to condition sharks to respond to selected patterns.

**BULL SHARKS**

*The bull shark is perhaps one of the most dangerous species of sharks. Known by many different common names, this animal has been linked to attacks around the world including some that have occurred deep inland in freshwater rivers and lakes.*

*INDO-PACIFIC LEMON SHARK (left)*

## Shark Attacks

The greatest fear of sharks is the fear of being attacked, in part due to the late Peter Benchley's novel and the movie *Jaws*. The International Shark Attack File (ISAF), maintained at the Florida Museum of Natural History at the University of Florida, compiles all data from reported attacks by sharks around the world. The driving force to create the file came from the United States Office of Naval Research in a quest to better understand shark attacks at the end of World War II. The original file was kept at the Smithsonian Institution in Washington, DC, and following short stays at a number of other institutions was eventually transferred to the Florida Museum under the aegis of the American Elasmobranch Society.

*GREAT WHITE SHARK*

worldwide with only seven fatalities. In 2005 that total dropped to 58 confirmed attacks with four fatalities, two in Australia, one in the United States, and one in Vanuatu in the Pacific. The ISAF further notes that 2005 was the fifth consecutive year that the number of unprovoked attacks has dropped. By comparison, the ISAF reported 18 fatalities from dogs and 15 fatalities from snakes, in 2004, just in the United States! The International Shark Attack File's website notes that 'The number of serious attacks in 2000-2005, as measured by fatality rate (8.5%), has been lower than that of the decade of the 1990's (12.7%), continuing a century-long trend reflective of advances in beach safety practices and medical treatment, and increased public awareness of avoiding potentially dangerous situations.'

Records of shark attacks date back to the 1500s. Nearly 3200 reports have been assembled. Scientists continually update the files and evaluate the statistics to decipher patterns and better understand when, where, and under what circumstances attacks occur.

The trends that have emerged suggest that shark attacks are indeed very rare. For example, in 2004, the ISAF recorded 65 unprovoked attacks that were confirmed to have occurred

A favorite comparison to make is between the probability of being struck by lightning and being attacked by a shark. The ISAF's analysis of deaths from lightning strikes in the US from 1959-2003 showed an average of 41.5 deaths from lightning strikes per year. During the same 44-year time span, there were only 22 deaths from shark attacks.

The US Navy worked with nurse sharks and was able to train them to retrieve items thrown to the bottom of a large pool and return them to the scientist 'trainer.' These early studies were captured on black and white film and are still exciting to view. Many other conditioning experiments have been undertaken to study various sensory systems and have shown that these animals may be much more capable of higher brain functions than we might expect.

Indeed, many years ago scientists in the Pacific, including a legendary behaviorist, Dr. Don Nelson, recorded on film displays from sharks that occurred immediately prior to an attack (termed 'agonistic displays'). Gray reef sharks could be provoked into giving the display and then into attacking scientists when they entered the area that the animals seemed to regard as their own. Other attack behaviors are less well studied.

We are still not clear what provokes a shark to attack a human. Some have speculated that surfers – often attacked by sharks – may appear in silhouette very similar to a seal or sea lion resting on the surface, though there is not strong agreement with such interpretations.

*GALAPAGOS SHARKS*

*Coloration in sharks is widely varied. Many display a deep gray color, often with very lightly colored undersides. When viewed from the surface, the dark upper body tends to blend in with the bottom or ocean depths. The light color of the underside, when viewed from beneath the animal, blends in well with the lighter surface of the water.*

*OCEANIC WHITETIP SHARK*

*Other fish may actually co-exist with sharks in symbiotic relationships. The remora ('shark sucker') frequently hitches a ride by attaching to sharks with a dorsal fin that acts like a suction cup. The remora may help to reduce the population of external parasites, serving the sharks like aquatic vacuum cleaners. They may benefit as well by feeding off scraps that are left behind when the shark feeds.*

Whether a shark attack is a directed attack, an accidental encounter, or a case of mistaken identity is not known.

We have seen certain reproductive behaviors that also seem to suggest some more advanced social organization in groups of nurse sharks, often regarded as a very social species of shark. Males often assist one another in mating events for reasons that we do not yet understand. There also appears to be some social structure, with a few males who are more dominant than others.

Some sharks also coexist with other fish in relationships that scientists term 'symbiotic' relationships – mutually beneficial. The remora – 'shark sucker' – is a fish whose dorsal fin is modified to allow it to attach to another fish, often a shark, and travel along, wherever its host travels. It appears that the remora feeds off the leftovers from a shark's meal and may, in turn, remove external parasites that may be attached to a shark. Sharks seem to be able to recognize and tolerate the remoras in exchange for the parasite removal services they perform.

It is clear from all of these studies that we have barely begun to understand these animals. But what we are learning is showing that their behaviors are far more complex than just feeding and attacking, and reproducing.

## How do Sharks Reproduce?

One aspect of shark biology that has been elusive to study has been reproduction and reproductive behavior. Though some smaller species have successfully reproduced in captivity, few of the larger species have been successful, in part because many of the larger sharks are harder to keep in captivity. In fact, only recently was a white shark held in captivity for a significant time. It was a juvenile female, which was released from captivity in the Monterey Bay Aquarium, California, in early 2005 after nearly six months in captivity when it began to prey upon other captive sharks. For those large species that do survive well in captivity and attempt to mate, few animals have been successful in giving birth.

In 1991 we began a study of mating behavior and reproductive biology of nurse sharks in the Florida Keys. It seems that some areas in the Keys had been known for shark mating for many years, in fact dating back to stories in magazine articles around 1860. This is probably because the waters of the Keys are very shallow and clear, and sharks near shore are easier to observe than sharks in deeper or dirtier water. Prior to our work, no systematic study of shark mating in the wild had been reported.

To understand the behaviors associated with mating in sharks, it should be understood that fertilization in sharks is internal, similar to many other vertebrate species. Males possess a pair of structures as modifications to their pelvic fins called 'claspers', which are inserted into a female during mating. Sperm passes through the clasper into the female where fertilization occurs. In nurse sharks, once an egg is fertilized, an egg case is produced that surrounds the egg. The embryonic shark develops within the egg case until the egg hatches

*NURSE SHARKS MATING*

*The pelvic fins of male sharks are modified to form structures called claspers. These reproductive structures are placed inside a female during mating and sperm is passed through the claspers into the female's reproductive tract, where fertilization occurs.*

### NEW-BORN LEMON SHARK

*Mating behaviors have been studied in only a few species. Some models suggest that males may travel together seeking females with whom they can mate. Similarly females often aggregate in large numbers during the time when the young sharks are born. What determines which males will be acceptable to certain females is still unknown. But it is clear that some species of sharks await the 'right' mate and their behaviors prior to mating may be as complex as those of animals considered more advanced.*

inside the mother. The empty egg case is shed shortly after the embryo hatches, and the young shark is born shortly thereafter. Some species of sharks may lay the eggs once they are fertilized. Other species actually develop a placenta that attaches the growing embryo to the mother's uterus during embryonic growth, similar to human development.

These strategies differ greatly from those of most other fish. In those species, females release huge quantities of eggs into the water and males release huge quantities of sperm during the time of spawning. These species invest their energy in producing large numbers of sperm and eggs and rely on percentages to produce more offspring. Sharks, instead, use internal fertilization and make their energy investment through the internal development of a comparatively smaller number of young.

Before mating occurs, mates must be selected. How this is achieved in most species is not clearly understood, but we are certain that in nurse sharks, the female makes the choice. Once she has 'chosen' her mate, the male must grip the female's pectoral fin in his mouth and insert his clasper into the female so that mating can be successful. Gripping the female – the shark's version of a 'hug' – seems to be a critical step. Several males may simultaneously compete for this grip. If the grip is not effective, the mating attempt will fail. Once mating is complete, the male will depart, though he may return and attempt to mate again at a later time.

Our studies have shown that females mate every two years and are reproductively active for a period that may be as short as just two weeks during the year that they mate. If females are to be successful and actually become pregnant, they must mate frequently during that short time. Furthermore, they may select more than one male during a mating 'season' to ensure that they are reproductively successful. Males, on the other hand, return to mate every year.

*SHORT-FINNED MAKO SHARK*

*Mako sharks are among the fastest swimming sharks. Their great speed enables them to chase down such fast-moving prey as tuna, mackerel and swordfish. Their antics when hooked on rod and reel make them one of the few shark species that is considered a 'game fish' by international game fishing organizations.*

Each female nurse shark may give birth to between 20 and 30 young sharks (a 'litter' of sharks) every time she becomes pregnant. Each of these litters may have several fathers, often four to six. This reproductive strategy ensures that females mate successfully and it also gives nurse shark litters some genetic diversity. Other species of sharks may not produce nearly as many 'pups' in a litter and many species produce only one or two offspring during each successful pregnancy.

While these behaviors are well documented for nurse sharks, few other species have been studied in the field. Their mechanisms of mate

*EGG CASE OF HORN SHARK*

*Different shark species give birth to their offspring in different ways. Some females lay eggs, often attached to structures on the sea floor, which eventually hatch and release the young. Other species develop a placenta, an attachment to the mother that nourishes the young during gestation. Still others produce eggs that develop inside the female, hatch inside the female, and some time after hatching the egg cases are shed and the young are born.*

*PREGNANT LEMON SHARK (right)*

selection and their mating behaviors may be different. We believe that the nurse shark will serve as the model shark-mating system, and we expect to see some similar activities in other species. We also expect to see some very different, unique, and species-specific behaviors in other species once mating grounds are determined for other species, and animals can be studied during these sensitive times. We have seen that our presence with video cameras and other scientific tools has actually often interrupted these behaviors, and we have recently worked with management authorities to close our study site during the times of mating to protect behaviors that can be interrupted by human activities.

## How Long are Sharks Pregnant?

The five-month gestation period for nurse sharks is actually very short for sharks. Many other species are pregnant for much longer periods. The common spiny dogfish is thought to carry its young for 20 to 24 months before giving birth. Some deep-water species are though to have gestation periods as long as 3.5 years, a very long time to be pregnant!

If we combine all of these various aspects of the life history of sharks – growth, aging, and reproduction – we see a group of animals that grow slowly, reproduce late in life, and produce relatively few offspring in each reproductive cycle. While these characteristics have served sharks well for most of their existence on earth, it leaves them vulnerable when their populations become the target of intense fishing pressures.

# Sharks & the Environment

## Are Sharks Valuable?

The value of sharks to the environment is similar to the role of any animal that is considered a top-level predator (an 'apex' predator). Though they reside at the top of the marine food chain and prey upon virtually any oceanic species, they also prey on sick and injured animals, animals that for some reason cannot escape. If these animals are diseased, then their elimination by sharks prevents the spread of disease. If they are genetically weak animals and they are eliminated by sharks before they can reproduce, those weaker genes are eliminated from the population and subsequent generations are made that much stronger.

This is natural selection at work, survival of the fittest. The argument is not new and not unique to sharks. The great cats of the Serengeti Plains in Africa perform similar functions for the many species of grazing animals that comprise one of the most complex ecosystems on earth.

Sharks have a great commercial value and are highly sought by fishermen around the world. In many countries, particularly in the Orient, they are prized for their fins, the major ingredient of shark fin soup. Too often the fins are removed from sharks and the remainder of the animal is thrown back into the sea, often still alive, only to sink to the bottom where they die. If the entire animal is taken and thoroughly processed, there is actually very little left to be discarded.

Prior to the chemical synthesis of vitamin A in the laboratory, there was a worldwide fishery for sharks because their livers are naturally rich

*BLUE SHARK FINS DRYING AT JAPANESE PRODUCTION CENTER*

*Worldwide, shark fisheries have intensified in recent decades and the advances in fisheries technology have placed these top-level predators under stresses they had never before faced in their 400 million years of existence. Drift gill nets, the practice of 'finning' live sharks and discarding the still-living carcasses without their fins, and the sheer efficiency of modern fishing techniques have placed populations of sharks that were once thought to be endless at peril for their very existence.*

*SILKY SHARKS (left)*

### TIGER SHARK

*The tiger shark is a large predatory species that has been reputed to eat almost anything including sea turtles, marine birds, license plates and suits of armor! They usually feed in shallow waters at night, and keep to deeper water during the day. The coloration of juveniles is intricate, with beautiful vertical bars that rival those of its namesake.*

in oils that contain high concentrations of vitamin A. Sharks were once heavily fished so that their livers could be processed to extract and purify the vitamin A, which was then added to milk to ensure that growing children received adequate amounts of this vitamin in their diet. That fishery has largely disappeared since synthetic versions have been available for nearly 50 years.

Shark meat, when properly processed, is excellent and has often been the fare of fish and chips. Shark skin can be tanned to prepare a fine grade of leather, though few tanneries have discovered the secrets of how to remove the dermal denticles to prepare the skin for tanning. The teeth have some commercial value as jewelry, and the entire jaws are often prized by collectors. In recent years, even the cartilage from the skeleton has been sought for its purported anti-cancer properties, though controlled scientific studies have largely rejected these claims. All uses considered, there is very little left to be discarded from a captured shark if every usable part is recovered. Unfortunately this is seldom the case and only selected parts are used by most commercial fisheries.

Sharks have very few natural enemies. Other sharks, many of the great toothed whales, and, while sharks are young and small, large groupers or sea bass, are their principal enemies. But their greatest natural enemy is not even an aquatic animal; it is man.

*GREAT WHITE SHARK*

The fisheries that target sharks have been very effective. There are many cases where local populations of sharks have been almost eliminated after only a few years of fishing pressure. Biologists worry that shark populations will have a very difficult time recovering from over-fishing, especially those species that are not migratory and can't escape local fishing pressure. Since they grow so slowly, mature very late in their lives, and do not produce many offspring when they do reproduce, they are potentially

*BLACKTIP SHARK*

*International conservation organizations are now crafting legislation for many shark species, some once considered pests because of their sheer numbers, which would provide them some protection from fishing pressures, in the hope that their numbers will be replenished.*

at risk unless they receive some legislative protection.

Many countries already impose fishing limits for sharks. They have begun to regulate the numbers of sharks that can be taken by both sport fishers and commercial fishers alike. Some regulations also control the types of sharks that can be taken and when they can be fished.

One problem that cannot be controlled by individual countries, however, is the migratory behavior of many species. Countries that share common borders may have very different attitudes about sharks and laws regulating shark fishing. Migrating sharks have no understanding of where laws exist that protect them. Their normal movements may take them from one area where they are protected to another region of the ocean where no such protection exists.

The only hope for protecting these important animals into the future is from worldwide recognition of their vulnerability and worldwide agreement to protect them. Some closely related species – sawfishes – are already regarded as endangered and international regulations have been created to protect them.

We have only recently begun to understand and believe that the ocean's resources are not endless and must be protected. Even species of sharks once regarded as pests – the spiny dogfish for example – have now been so severely over-fished that international regulations have been proposed to list them as endangered or threatened and ban their use or trade, worldwide.

The loss of apex predators has occurred in terrestrial habitats many times. Wolves, giant cats, and other animals that are threats to humans or domesticated animals have often been hunted to near elimination. The effect of their loss on other animals that they normally prey upon has been nearly catastrophic. Populations of prey animals have grown huge without their natural predators. Other food sources have been exploited by herds that have grown beyond their normal food supplies. Diseases have been allowed to run rampant because weaker animals now survive instead of being controlled by predators.

*CARIBBEAN REEF SHARKS*

*Sharks are often considered to be indiscriminate feeders, opportunistic fish that will feed on anything the sea has to offer. In fact most species seem to have preferred diets. Depending on their particular habits, they may prefer to chase down fish, or they may select slower-moving prey such as crustaceans including shrimps, crabs, and lobsters.*

**GRAY REEF SHARK**

*Sharks are widely distributed and are found in nearly all marine waters. They are encountered in shallow, nearshore waters as well as the open seas and from the tropics to the cold waters of the Arctic seas. The continuing development of deep-sea research vessels has shown that sharks also inhabit the deepest ocean depths. More as-yet-undiscovered species are likely to be found as this new technology is further refined.*

**TIGER SHARK (right)**

Nearly 75 per cent of the earth's surface is covered with water, most of it from the world's oceans, where the shark has been in control for nearly 400 million years. It is beyond imagination to believe that their dominance could be threatened by another predator in a mere 50 to 100 years, a predator who has yet to understand the harmony of nature's laws of coexistence.

What a sad thought to contemplate: an ocean without its most majestic and graceful inhabitant, a world without sharks... There is still time, and hope. The growing industry of ecotourism brings people into contact with animals that they may never otherwise encounter. While the industry also brings problems of its own from human presence in natural areas, it also brings some level of awareness and respect that might not occur otherwise.

In recent years, we have seen more and more 'shark dives' around the world, managed trips to see sharks in the wild. People who encounter sharks and come to understand that they are just another example of the wonderful diversity of organisms that exist on our earth are helping to spread the word that sharks deserve respect and protection. Education and understanding is again our only hope for protecting sharks for the remainder of time. We would do well to remember the words of Baba Dioum, a poet and former Director of Senegal's Agriculture Policy Unit, who concluded that, 'In the end

We will conserve only what we love,

We will love only what we understand,

We will understand only what we are taught...'

aging 6, 28, 38

ancestors 12, **13**

angel shark **15**, 18

attacks 25, 32-34

basking shark 18, **19**, 28

birth 36, 38

blacktip shark **24**, **44**

blacktip reef shark **5**

blue shark 28, **29**

breathing, respiration 9, 10, 22

bronze whaler (copper shark) **20**, 21

bull shark 14, **31**

Caribbean reef shark 28, **45**

carpet shark 18

conservation 44, 45

cookie-cutter shark 12

eggs 36, **38**

epaulette shark 18

eyes 7, 14, 22, **23**, 24, 25

fisheries **41**, 42, 44

feeding, food 9, 12, 18, 22, 21, 24, 25, 28, 31, 34, 41, 45

Galapagos shark **33**

gills 9, 10, 22

gray reef shark **22**, **25**, 33, **46**

great white shark **1**, **8**, 9, 12, 18, **21**, **32**, **43**

growth 6, 26-28, 36, 38

hammerhead shark 6, **14**, 17

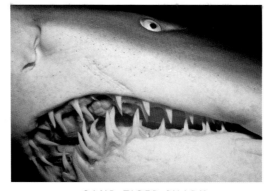

**SAND TIGER SHARK**

hearing 23, 24

horn shark 38

lemon shark **30**, 31, **36**, **39**

leopard shark **15**, 18

mako shark, short-finned **37**

mating 28, 34-38

migration 25, 28, 44

nurse shark **6**, 10, **27**, 28, **35**, 37, 38

oceanic whitetip shark **34**

pregnancy 37, 38

prey 12, 14, 17, 18, 21, 22, 23, 25, 37, 45

reproduction 6, 27, 34, 38, 41, 44

research 6, 32, 46

sandbar shark **4**, **5**, 28

sand tiger shark 18, **26**, **48**

saw shark 15

seven-gill shark **9**

silky shark **16**, **40**

silvertip shark **2**, **10**

skin 9, **11**, 18, 27

smell 22, 23, 25

tagging 26-29

teeth 9, 11, **12**, **13**

thresher shark 18

tiger shark **7**, **42**, **47**

vision 23, 24

whale shark **17**, 28

wobbegong shark **18**

zebra (leopard) shark **15**

BIOGRAPHY: Dr. Jeffrey C. Carrier is W.W. Diehl Trustees' Professor of Biology, Albion College, Albion, MI. Dr. Carrier has studied sharks for over 30 years, and is currently serving his second term as President of the American Elasmobranch Society. He and his students have appeared in many network and cable television programs, from National Geographic Explorer and Discovery Channel specials to Florida Public Television documentaries.

Photographs © 2006 Seapics.com by:

Jonathon Bird, front cover
Dan Burton, page: 19
Phillip Colla, pages: 23 bottom right, 43
Mark Conlin, pages: 2, 44
Ben Cropp Productions, page: 30
Jeremy Stafford-Deitsch, pages: 15 bottom right, 46
Steve Drogin, page: 10
C & M Fallows, pages: 21, 31
Saul Gonor, page: 15 top left
Howard Hall, pages: 38, 40
Makoto Hirose / e-Photography, page: 41
Paul Humann, page: back cover

Doug Perrine, pages: 1, 9, 11, 12, 18, 20, 23 top right, 24, 25, 26, 27, 28, 29, 33, 36, 37, 39
Jim Robinson, page: 22
Jeff Rotman, pages: 23 bottom left, 48
Norine Rouse, page: 35
Marty Snyderman, page: 15 top right
Nat Sumanatemeya, page: 5
Hiroyuki Tatsuuma / e-Photography, pages: 23 top le
Ray Troll, page: 13
Masa Ushioda, pages: 6, 7, 15 bottom left, 16, 34, 47
James D Watt, pages: 4, 8, 14, 17, 32, 42, 45